P9-EMG-210

creatures
of the sea

Sea Stars

Other titles in the series:

creatures of the sea

Sea Stars

Kris Hirschmann

**KIDHAVEN
PRESS**™

THOMSON

GALE™

San Diego • Detroit • New York • San Francisco • Cleveland
New Haven, Conn. • Waterville, Maine • London • Munich

For more information, contact
KidHaven Press
27500 Drake Rd.
Farmington Hills, MI 48331-3535
Or you can visit our Internet site at http://www.gale.com

LIBRARY OF CONGRESS CATALOGING-IN-PUBLICATION DATA

Hirschmann, Kris, 1967–
    Sea stars / by Kris Hirschmann.
      p. cm.—(Creatures of the sea)
Summary: Describes the physical characteristics, behavior, predators, and life cycle of the sea star, also known as the starfish.
    ISBN 0-7377-1362-3 (hardback : alk. paper)
1.Starfishes—Juvenile literature. [1. Starfishes.] I. Title. II. Series.
    QL384 .A8 H58 2003
    593 .9'3—dc21
                                    J
                                    593.93
    2002001389
                                    HIR
                                    c.1

$18.96

Printed in the United States of America

Table of Contents

Introduction

Symbols of the Sea

Up and down the West Coast of the United States, standing pools of water form during periods of low tide. These pools are called tide pools, and they are full of life.

Tide pools are popular among human visitors who want to watch and enjoy interesting ocean creatures without entering the sea. Crabs, fish, and sea anemones are part of the draw for these visitors. But the most popular tide pool residents are sea stars. With their colorful bodies and multiple arms, these animals delight and fascinate adults and children alike. They are so well liked, in fact, that they have become symbols of the sea in many cultures around the world.

Bright orange sea stars stand out in this tide pool in California.

Sea stars are not found only in West Coast tide pools. They live in every ocean on Earth—and *only* there. Sea stars cannot live in freshwater. But even though they are picky about their living conditions,

Two women examine colorful, puffy sea stars while snorkeling in shallow water.

sea stars thrive in the right environment. They reproduce quickly and create many new sea stars.

This is good news for scientists, who still have much to learn about sea stars. It is also good news for divers, snorkelers, shell collectors, aquarium owners, and other people who appreciate the beauty and behaviors of sea stars. Finally, it is good for the planet. Sea stars are keystone species in the ocean. This means that they are essential to the natural balance. If sea stars stay healthy, it will help the oceans to stay healthy too. So these star-shaped creatures are more than just symbols of the sea. They are its protectors as well.

Sea Star Anatomy

Sea stars are sometimes called "starfish." However, this term has fallen out of favor with scientists around the world because it is not accurate. Sea stars are not fish. They are members of the **echinoderm** family, which also includes sea urchins, sea cucumbers, sea lilies, and sand dollars.

The echinoderm family is large. It contains about six thousand separate species. Of these species, about sixteen hundred are true sea stars, also called **asteroids**. Scientists use the term "true sea stars" to separate asteroids from brittle stars and basket stars, which look like sea stars but are not.

Sea stars are common around the world. They live in every ocean on Earth and thrive in a wide range of temperatures. Some species of sea stars prefer the warm waters of the tropics, while others like the chilly seas far north and south of the equator. Most sea stars, however, are found in mild waters that range from fifty to seventy degrees Fahrenheit.

Sea stars are also common in many different regions of the ocean. Most sea stars are found in the shallow waters near land, living their lives in tide pools, on coastal reefs, or on rocky bottoms. But some prefer deeper waters. There are sea stars at all depths of the oceans, even in trenches that plunge miles below the sea's surface.

Anemones surround a sea star, one of many that live in warm, tropical water.

No matter where they live, sea stars are bottom dwellers. They spend their days and nights crawling around on the ocean floor. Most sea stars seek rock, coral, or other hard surfaces because it is easy to cling to these substances. A few types of sea stars prefer sand or mud.

Sea stars come in a wide range of sizes. The smallest sea stars are less than one inch across, while the largest can be more than three feet from tip to tip. But these extremes of size are not common. Most sea stars measure between six and twelve inches in width.

Sea stars also come in a wide range of colors. These animals may be solid red, orange, yellow,

Sea stars come in many sizes. Some are as large as a dinner plate (left) and some are as small as a hockey puck.

green, blue, brown, or purple. They may also be multicolored or have unusual patterns. One unusual species is nicknamed the "chocolate chip sea star" because of its coloring. This animal looks just like a chocolate chip cookie baked in the shape of a sea star.

The Sea Star Shape

The sea star body is **radially symmetrical**. This means that the sea star has a number of evenly spaced "arms," called **rays**, that poke outward from a central body. Almost all other animals are bilaterally symmetrical, which means that they have two more-or-less identical halves. So the sea star's body type is very unusual in the animal world.

Most sea stars have five rays spreading out from their body. But there are many exceptions to this rule. It is common for sea stars to have six, seven, eight, nine, eleven, even fifteen rays—or more. Sun stars, for example, a large species found near Europe, South America, and Antarctica, may have as many as fifty rays. It is also possible for individuals of a single species to have different numbers of rays. The bat star, for example, is usually a five-rayed species, but bat stars with three, four, six, seven, and eight rays are common in some areas.

Body size and ray shape are very different from species to species. Some sea stars have long slender arms with a small body holding them together. Other sea stars have short thick arms that join a large central body. And a few types of sea stars, including

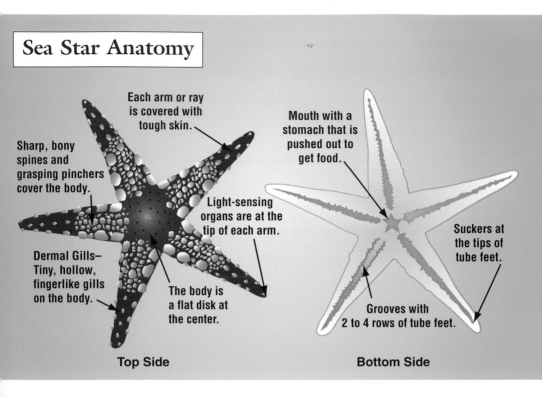

Sea Star Anatomy

Each arm or ray is covered with tough skin.

Sharp, bony spines and grasping pinchers cover the body.

Mouth with a stomach that is pushed out to get food.

Light-sensing organs are at the tip of each arm.

Dermal Gills—Tiny, hollow, fingerlike gills on the body.

The body is a flat disk at the center.

Suckers at the tips of tube feet.

Grooves with 2 to 4 rows of tube feet.

Top Side   **Bottom Side**

the yellow-and-orange pincushion star, have such big bodies and stubby arms that they look almost like giant sand dollars.

A Closer Look

A closer look at a sea star reveals many interesting features. The sea star's body is flattened, with a definite top and bottom. There is no head, but there is a mouth, located in the middle of the body on the bottom side of the sea star. The anus, a hole through which the sea star gets rid of waste, is found on the top side.

The sea star's top side has many other features as well. Most sea stars have sharp bony spines that help to protect them from **predators**. In some species, these spines are long and deadly looking. In other species, they are so short that they are difficult to see. And some species have no spines at all.

Many sea stars also have pinchers called **pedicellariae** on their top sides. A single sea star may have dozens of pairs of pedicellariae. Sea stars can use their pedicellariae to remove small objects that fall onto them. They can also use their pinchers to attack animals that come too close.

Dermal gills are another feature often found on sea stars' top sides. Dermal gills are small, delicate structures that start inside the sea star's body and stick up from the animal's surface. These organs help

Sea stars use their pinchers to fight off predators.

sea stars to breathe by taking oxygen from the water and releasing carbon dioxide gas. Little hairs inside the gills, called **cilia**, beat back and forth. The cilia create currents that carry new oxygen-rich water deep into the sea star and old water out of the animal through its gills.

Tube Feet

The most interesting feature on the bottom side of the sea star is **tube feet**. Each tube foot is tiny, but there are many of them. A sea star may have hundreds or even thousands of tube feet arranged in neat rows along its rays. Working together, the tube feet allow a sea star to travel slowly along the ocean floor.

The sea star controls its tube feet with water pressure. The sea star sucks in water through a filtered opening on the top of its body to fill special cavities in its body. Then it uses its muscles to pump the water into the tube feet. As the feet fill, they expand. Muscles in the foot wall then direct the movement of the fully extended foot. The muscles can also push water out of the foot to make it smaller. By alternately filling, using, and emptying different tube feet, the sea star can move in any direction it likes.

The sea star can also use its tube feet to cling to most hard surfaces. The tip of each tube foot can be used as a tiny suction cup. When hundreds of tube feet are sucking at the same time, it is almost impossible to pry the sea star loose from its perch.

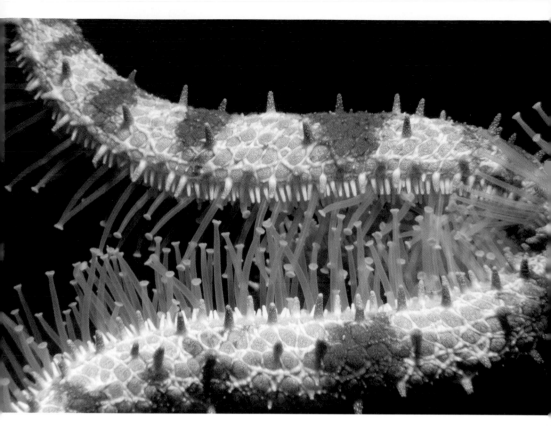

Hundreds of tiny tube feet move the sea star along the ocean floor.

Recent studies show that some sea stars also create an adhesive, or sticky substance, with their tube feet. This adhesive adds to the sea star's already impressive clinging power. Between its sucking and sticking abilities, a sea star is likely to stay exactly where it likes.

Sensing the World

Amazingly, a sea star manages to coordinate its many feet (and the rest of its movements and functions) without the help of a brain. Although sea stars have

The tip of a sea star's ray senses light, which helps it detect the shadow of a passing predator.

nerves running throughout their bodies, there is no brain to control all the nerves.

Though a sea star has no brain, it does have senses, and it uses these senses to find its way around the ocean floor and keep itself fed. A sea star has a well-developed sense of touch that helps it to find shelter and prey. It has a sense of taste that helps it identify food. And it has a light-sensing organ at the tip of each ray. The light-sensing organs do not see, but they can tell a sea star if the shadow of a predator passes overhead. They can also guide the sea star into dimly lit crevices or toward the open, sunny sea floor.

A sea star has all the equipment it needs to make its way through the world. However, this animal's brainless state ensures that it cannot think or plan in even the most basic way. Instead, the sea star seems designed to wander the seas looking for food. It is not a complicated life. But it works well for the sea star, which has enjoyed life on Earth for more than 400 million years already and will probably be around for many more to come.

The Hunter and the Hunted

Most sea stars are **carnivores**, which means that they eat other animals to survive. Most are also predators, which means that they hunt and kill their food.

Different sea stars prefer different types of food. Certain species live almost entirely on clams and other **bivalves**, animals with hinged, two-halved shells. Some species enjoy crabs and shrimp. Others prefer worms, fish, sponges, or coral. And then there are some species that do not seem to have any food preferences. These sea stars eat anything they can catch and stuff into their mouths. In fact, scientists found one large sea star whose stomach contained the body of a sea bird.

Slow but Steady

The sea star is a slow but steady hunter. Moving at a top speed of about twenty inches per minute, this animal creeps around its ocean home in a constant

A dead goosefish provides a tasty meal for sea stars.

search for food. It uses its senses of touch and taste as it goes, looking for signs of prey. Some sea stars eat constantly as they move, feeding on the tiny animals that live along the ocean floor. Sea stars that eat larger prey may spend days seeking their next meal.

The hunting path of a sea star can seem random, since this animal may change direction quickly and without turning. The sea star can do this because its body has no front or back end. Any ray can lead. Thus, a sea star usually sets off in whatever direction it likes, using the ray that lies in that direction as its leading arm. When the sea star wants to go a different way, it simply switches to a new ray and heads off on a new course without ever rotating its body.

This hunting process may be slow, but it works. Sea stars seldom have trouble finding the food they need. It may take some time, but a hungry sea star will always find a meal.

Getting Food to the Mouth

Most sea stars eat by bringing food to their mouths. The rays are not flexible enough to do this job, however, so sea stars have come up with many interesting ways of keeping themselves fed.

The simplest technique is bottom-feeding. All sea stars have grooves running along the bottom side of each ray. In bottom-feeding species, these grooves are lined with cilia. A sea star spreads itself flat on the ocean floor, bringing its rays into contact with as

A spiky sea star prepares to eat a section of coral by wrapping itself around it.

much surface area as possible. Next it beats its cilia in an organized pattern to set up currents in the water. These currents lift tiny creatures from the ocean floor, then sweep them down the grooves and into the sea star's mouth.

Other sea stars catch food with mucus. These species lift their rays off the sea floor and then squirt long, sticky strands of mucus from between their tube feet. They let these strands drift in the water. After a while, they draw the strands in and eat any small animals that have gotten stuck.

A few species even use their pedicellariae as hunting weapons. If a fish or another small creature bumps into certain sea stars, the pedicellariae grab it and hold it tight. The sea star transfers the captured prey from one set of pedicellariae to the next, moving it across the body and toward the mouth. When the prey gets within range of the mouth, the sea star gobbles down its meal.

Incredible Stomachs

The most amazing sea star feeding technique involves something called external digestion. Some types of sea stars have the ability to poke their stomachs out through their mouths and digest things outside of their bodies. Coral-feeding and sponge-eating sea stars eat in this way. These sea stars simply settle on top of their prey, stick out their stomachs, and start digesting their food right away.

Sea stars that eat clams, mussels, and other bivalves also use external digestion. Before they can begin the digestive process, however, they must get to their prey's body. Bivalves' soft bodies are protected by two shell halves that are held closed by a strong muscle. To reach its meal, a sea star wraps its body around the shells and applies sucking power with its many tube feet. It pulls steadily until the prey's muscle tires and its shells crack open.

The sea star does not need much of a crack to get to its prey. An opening measuring just one-tenth of a millimeter is enough to let in part of the sea star's stomach. With a tiny bit of its stomach inside the prey's shell, the sea star releases digestive juices

A sea star uses its tube feet to weaken a mussel and crack open its shell.

that weaken its prey. As the prey weakens, its muscle power decreases. After a while the shell pops open and the sea star can enjoy its meal.

Small bivalves are easier to open than large ones. Most sea stars do not hesitate to tackle an especially big meal, however. A sea star that finds a large clam or mussel wraps itself around its prey as usual and begins to pull. If the opponents are evenly matched, the battle may go on for days before the prey tires and opens its shells wide enough for the sea star's stomach to get inside.

The Sea Star as Prey

Although sea stars eat many animals, few animals eat sea stars. With their bony skeletons and spiny skins, most sea stars do not make a good meal. Also, because they do not carry much muscle or fat, they are not very nutritious. So most of the time, sea stars go about their business undisturbed.

However, a few animals do eat sea stars when they get the chance. Some fish snack on these creatures. Some large ocean snails count on sea stars as part of their diet. And sea stars may even be dangerous to each other: Large sea stars often eat smaller ones.

For this reason, sea stars have a variety of defenses that protect them from predators. For such a slow-moving creature, the best way to stay safe is simply not to be seen in the first place. To accomplish this goal, many sea stars match their skin color

An otter gnaws on a sea star, although it probably will not be a satisfying meal.

to their surroundings. Others partly bury themselves in sand or mud to keep their bodies out of sight.

If a sea star is seen and attacked despite its best efforts to stay hidden, stronger defenses are needed. Some sea stars use their pedicellariae to pinch an attacker. Others use sharp spines to jab any animal that gets too close. In some species, the spines and pedicellariae even produce a mild venom. This venom is

The five shortest rays are going through the process of regeneration.

not strong enough to kill an attacker, but it can cause enough pain to make a hungry predator back off.

When all else fails, a sea star may try to escape by running away. Because sea stars are so slow, this tactic is not effective against fish and other fast-moving creatures. But a sea star *can* sometimes outrun snails and other sea stars.

Regeneration

Sometimes a sea star's defenses fail and it is partly eaten. But even then, a sea star may survive and eventually return to its original form. This is possible because of an ability called **regeneration**. Regeneration means that a sea star can regrow missing parts of its body. As long as most of the body disk and at least one ray are undamaged, a sea star can replace everything that is destroyed in an attack or an accident.

Life in the ocean is not easy, so sea stars often lose rays. It is therefore common to find sea stars that have several mature rays and one or two short nubs. The nubs are brand-new rays that the sea star is growing to replace its lost parts. It takes about a year for these new rays to reach adult size. When fully grown, the new rays look exactly like the old ones.

Built to Survive

Between their hunting skills, their defensive tricks, and their ability to regenerate lost parts, sea stars are well equipped to survive in the ocean. Although sea stars are simple animals, they are certainly among the most successful creatures living in the seas today.

The Life of a Sea Star

Sea stars do not age, as most animals do. So in theory, it is possible for a sea star to live forever. Reality, however, is a bit different. Many things, including predators, illness, starvation, and injury, can and do kill sea stars. Most sea stars live no more than three or four years before falling prey to one of these situations.

Between birth and death, a sea star's life follows a cycle of development, adulthood, and eventually parenthood. It is this cycle that produces new sea stars and keeps populations steady.

The Larval Phase

Sea stars begin their lives as tiny **larvae** that look nothing like their adult relatives. The larvae have

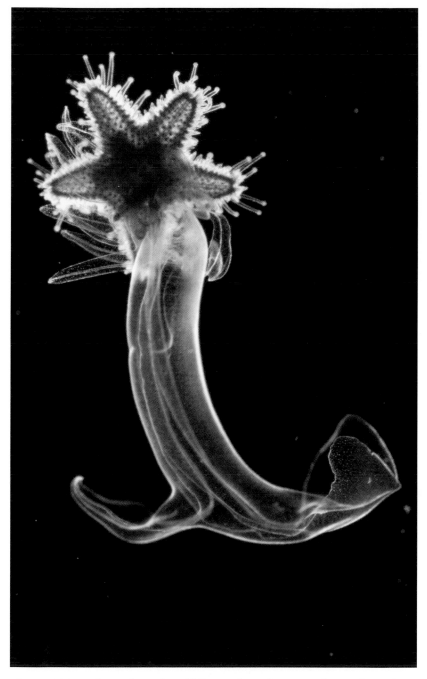

A sea star detaches itself from its clear sack, a sign that it is near the end of the larva stage.

oddly shaped bodies with many projecting arms. They are bilaterally symmetrical, meaning they have two similar halves. They also have a front and rear like most animals, instead of a top and bottom like adult sea stars.

Sea star larvae develop in open water and immediately become part of the plankton, a population of very small plants and animals that floats near the ocean's surface. As soon as it enters this population, a sea star larva begins to hunt. It eats as many of its tiny neighbors as it can catch. As it eats, it becomes bigger and stronger.

Although the plankton stage is a time of great growth and opportunity for a sea star larva, it is also a time of great danger. Sea stars are not the only hunters roaming the plankton. There are many other small but hungry creatures searching for food in the same region. And most of these creatures do not hesitate to eat a sea star larva. Plankton is also the main food source of some large animals, including some whales and sharks. These creatures can swallow huge amounts of plankton in a single gulp. Between predators both small and large, most sea star larva are eaten within days of their birth.

Becoming an Adult

If a sea star larva survives the dangers of the planktonic life, it eventually gets big and heavy enough to start its journey toward the ocean floor. In warm waters, it takes about three weeks for a larva to reach

Sea stars are in danger when they live among plankton (pictured) because it is food for many predators.

this stage. Cold-water larvae do not grow as fast, so it may take as much as three months for sea star larvae in cooler climates to become large enough to sink to the ocean floor.

Surviving the plankton stage is an important first step for a sea star. But it is no guarantee of success. Because the plankton drifts freely with the ocean currents, many sea star larvae end up in regions where they cannot survive. The sea floor may be too deep, or there may not be enough food of the right type to keep an adult sea star fed. If a sea star larva finds itself in any of these situations after it leaves the plankton, it will die.

Some sea star larvae, however, both survive the plankton and find themselves in favorable conditions when they settle to the ocean floor. If this is the case, a larva attaches itself to a rock or a piece of coral with a sucker and begins an incredible transformation. It takes only a few hours for the larva to completely change the shape of its body and turn itself into a miniature adult. When the change is complete, the new sea star leaves its rocky perch and sets off across the ocean floor in search of food. Its adult life has begun.

Spawning

It takes most sea stars one or two years to reach maturity after they become adult in form. When maturity is reached, it is time for a sea star to reproduce and create new sea stars.

Nearly all sea stars reproduce by **spawning**. This means that females release eggs and males release sperm into the water around the same time. Most sea stars are nowhere near each other when they spawn. The eggs and sperm meet up by chance as they float through the ocean.

Spawning usually happens in the spring or early summer. At these times of the year, light and temperature conditions bring about chemical changes in a female sea star's body. The chemical changes cause the female to release eggs. Different species of sea stars release different numbers of eggs, but the numbers are usually large: A sea star may release more than two million eggs at a time.

A chocolate-chip sea star is about to spawn, or release sperm or eggs.

Once released, the female's eggs drift away on the ocean currents. With a little luck they will drift past male sea stars, who sense the eggs and release sperm in response. The sperm then fertilize the eggs, which eventually grow into brand-new larvae.

Although most sea stars leave the mating process to chance, a few take care of their eggs and babies. Some sea stars attach their eggs to the ocean floor and protect them with their bodies until they hatch. Others carry their larvae inside their bodies until they change into tiny adults. Of all sea stars, cold-water species are the most likely to protect their young in these ways. Scientists believe that the conditions in colder water make protection necessary for the young sea stars' survival.

Reproduction by Splitting

Some types of sea stars can reproduce without spawning. To create new life, these sea stars simply split in half, right down the center of the body disk. Each half then begins to regrow its missing pieces. Before long, there are two healthy sea stars instead of one. The two new individuals may not look exactly the same, though: The new sea stars may have a different number of rays from the original.

A sea star called the Pacific comet, found along the west coasts of Mexico and California, has an especially unusual way of splitting itself. This five-rayed sea star holds tight to a firm surface with four of its rays while the other ray pulls itself away from the

A sea star detaches one of its rays, which starts the process of creating a whole new individual.

body. The sea star's flesh is stretched tighter and tighter until finally the pulling ray breaks off of the body disk. The ray then crawls away to start a new life on its own. Soon a body disk and four tiny ray stubs sprout from the broken end of the ray.

Population Explosions

During a sea star's life, population levels usually remain steady. Sometimes, however, sea star populations can explode. This happens when natural conditions change in a way that allows more sea stars than usual to survive.

In one case, oysters in the northeast United States provided so much food that the local sea star population began to grow. In an attempt to fix the problem, oystermen chopped the sea stars' bodies in half and dumped the pieces back into the sea. The oystermen thought they were killing the sea stars. But in fact, they were creating new ones. The sea star population exploded as the chopped-off pieces regrew their missing parts.

Sea star populations also may increase for unknown reasons. The crown-of-thorns sea star, a large tropical species that feeds on coral, is particularly well known for doing this. Scientists often discover that a previously calm reef has been overrun by huge numbers of crown-of-thorns stars. The sea stars feast on the coral for several years before a falling food supply forces their population back down to normal levels.

The crown-of-thorns sea star reproduces rapidly when it has a large supply of coral to eat.

The Future of Sea Stars

It is not surprising that sea stars are prone to population explosions. As a keystone species in the seas, sea stars not only affect the conditions around them. They also are affected themselves by any changes that occur in their environment.

Today, human activities and waste products are changing the oceans of the world. No one knows for sure what these changes will do to sea stars. But like every other ocean-dwelling species, sea stars are sure to be affected.

Fortunately, nature has designed sea stars to be very tough. In their long history on Earth, sea stars have survived many natural changes. They probably will survive man-made changes, too. Chances are good that the sea star life cycle will continue to go on throughout all the world's oceans, just as it does today.

Glossary

asteroid: A name that scientists use to refer to true sea stars.

bivalves: Clams, mussels, oysters, and other animals with hinged, two-halved shells.

carnivore: Any animal that eats only the flesh of other animals.

cilia: Tiny hairs that beat rhythmically to create water currents.

dermal gills: Organs that release carbon dioxide and take in oxygen.

echinoderm: The family of animals that includes sea stars, sea urchins, sea cucumbers, and sea lilies.

larvae: Newly hatched sea stars, before they change into their adult form.

pedicellariae: Tiny pinchers found on the top sides of some sea stars.

predator: Any animal that hunts other animals to survive.

radial symmetry: Evenly arranged around a central point.

ray: One of the "arms" that is attached to the sea star's central body disk.

regeneration: The ability to regrow missing parts.

spawning: Releasing eggs and sperm into the water.

tube feet: Hollow, fleshy tubes with suction-cup ends that line the bottom of a sea star's rays.

For Further Exploration

Books

Gordon Hendler, *Sea Stars, Sea Urchins, and Allies: Echinoderms of Florida and the Caribbean*. Washington, DC: Smithsonian Institution Press, 1995. This book is written for adults, but it contains more than a hundred beautiful full-color pictures of sea stars and their relatives.

Sandra Romashko, *The Shell Book: The Complete Guide to Collecting and Identifying with a Special Section on Starfish and Other Sea Creatures*. Miami, FL: Windward Publications, 1974. Learn all about collecting sea shells and sea star skeletons in this interesting book.

Christiane Kump Tibbitts, *Seashells, Crabs, and Sea Stars*. Minocqua, WI: Northword Press, 1996. Learn a little bit about sea stars and some of their seaside neighbors.

Periodical

James A. Sugar, "Starfish Threaten Pacific Reefs," *National Geographic*, March 1970. This article tells the story of a crown-of-thorns infestation.

Websites

Life on the Rocky Shore (www.library.thinkquest. org). A fun site all about tide pools and the creatures that live in them, including sea stars. Students can take a sea star quiz or solve a sea star crossword puzzle.

Phylum Echinodermata (www.fig.cox.miami.edu). This site has a good illustration showing the many different forms a newly hatched sea star takes as it grows into an adult.

index

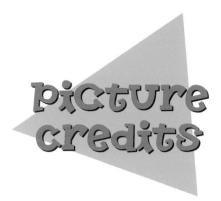

picture credits

Cover photo: © Flip Nicklin/Minden Pictures

© Fred Bavendam/Minden Pictures, 37

© Brandon D. Cole/CORBIS, 39

© Stephen Frink/CORBIS, 8, 15

© Fred McConnaughey/Photo Researchers, Inc., 28

© Mark Newman/Photo Researchers, Inc., 12

Brandy Noon, 14

© Gregory Ochocki/Photo Researchers, Inc., 11

© Matthew Oldfield, Scubazoo, SPL, Photo Researchers, Inc., 35

© Jeffrey L. Rotman/CORBIS, 17, 18, 21, 23

© Galen Rowell/CORBIS, 7

© Kennan Ward/CORBIS, 27

© Douglas P. Wilson; Frank Lane Picture Agency/CORBIS, 31, 33

© Lawson Wood/CORBIS, 25

about the author

Kris Hirschmann has written more than sixty books for children, mostly on science and nature topics. She is the president of The Wordshop, a business that provides a wide variety of writing and editorial services. She holds a bachelor's degree in psychology from Dartmouth College in Hanover, New Hampshire.

Hirschmann lives just outside of Orlando, Florida, with her husband, Michael.